SEX POSITION FOR COUPLES:

A KAMA SUTRA AND TANTRIC SEX GUIDE FOR BEGINNERS TO AMPLIFY PLEASURE WITH YOUR POSITIONS AND INCREASE THE PASSION IN YOUR RELATIONSHIP

Contents

Introduction

For any healthy relationship to prosper, the couple must indulge in healthy sex. Sex isn't just one of the basic primal needs. But at the same time, it is the way to create a bond that strengthens the two people who are a part of it.

When we talk of sex, the kind of topic it encompasses is huge and wide. Not everyone gets to enjoy the best level of sex which infers that there is something which some of us miss out on. This aspires to help you reconnect with your inner sexual drive. Learn the best ways by which you can maximize your sexual potential and live every fantasy.

With these expert tips, you are sure to find a difference in your bedroom life and as a couple; you are much more likely to grow. The physical attraction you feel is a very strong component in any relationship, and as long as you don't feel the need to ravish each other, the sparks won't fly.

So, it is time to shed all inhibitions as far as getting intimate is concerned. This isn't meant solely for reading purposes. It will take you on a ride which will unravel the different layers of your body and help you understand your true sexual drive.

All relationships will come across bumps in the road. It is a normal and natural thing. When you are working toward true intimacy, you will work as a team. You will be compassionate when trying to solve a problem. Not only will you take your thoughts into consideration, but also your partner's. You should not be competing about who is right, rather working together to find a solution that is mutually beneficial. Having an intimate relationship with someone will indeed affect you on a physical, emotional, and mental level. You will be sharing your whole self with someone. When you do this, you are allowing them to have an impact on you in every way. This means you need to be careful with whom you become intimate with. Later in this, we will intuition and compatibility; when we do, we will hit on this more.

When we enter into a new relationship, we start to learn about the good and bad sides of a person. Showing yourself and exposing what you truly believe is a step in the right direction when trying to attain a truly intimate relationship. Know that when you express yourself in a raw way, the reaction may not be what you expect. Obviously, you want your partner to be understanding and supportive, but remember that it goes both ways. So, when they are expressing themselves, think about your reactions and how it is affecting the person you are developing feelings for.

Taking the time to look at your differences is very important. It can help you understand if the relationship is worth moving forward with. Having some beliefs that don't line up is fine; however, if you are truly opposites, it will likely lead to bigger problems down the road. Some differences can help us grow and evolve while others can be complete deal-breakers. Finding these things out, in the beginning, can help you avoid heartache and wasting your time.

Chapter 1-   Tantric Techniques

It is no secret that poor sexual performance is to blame for a lot of problems in relationships and marriages. This is a sad fact considering the importance that sex plays in any relationship. The availability of countless sex tips in the modern world has done little to help men to last longer in bed. It has done nothing to increase the frequency of orgasms that couples have and neither has it helped people to be happy. Tantric principles of sexuality form the basic foundations of any great sexual performance and satisfaction. They not only allow men to last longer in bed and have better sexual performance in the bedroom, but they are also great in increasing intimacy in the bedroom. Here is what you should know about these principles.

The powerful techniques of tantric sexuality are not new to the world and it is thus surprising that very few people know of them. Fewer people apply these techniques in their daily lives and thus one of the major reasons why people never maximize their emotional satisfaction and sensual pleasures during sexual intercourse. This is what tantric principles of sexuality help people to achieve. When properly applied, these principles are great at enabling couples to develop the skills not only to having mind-blowing orgasms but also of having lasting orgasms as many times as they wish.

Studies have always shown that the key to lasting longer in bed and having a great sexual performance in the bedroom lies in taking things slow. This is what every woman wants and the only known shortcut to better sexual satisfaction. However, the modern lifestyle has placed an emphasis on immediate self-gratification such that all that people seek is an immediate pleasure and taking shortcuts in life. While this might be great for some aspects of our lives, it does nothing towards helping people enjoy sex more. It is not only a leading cause of premature ejaculation and other dysfunctions of the sexual organs but it also robs sex of its true essence of pleasure and intimacy.

Tantric sexual techniques emphasize on heightening sexual stimulation and sensation by taking a spiritual approach to sex and satisfaction. By enabling couples to connect both their bodies and minds, couples are able to expand the boundaries of sexual pleasure and satisfaction in the bedroom. Since the techniques take a spiritual and mental approach to sexual intercourse, they usually enhance a man's calmness and tranquility during sex and thus allowing him to be in better control of his arousal levels. As such, it is possible for a man to prevent premature ejaculation and last longer in bed.

It often seems complicated to get a woman to have a screaming orgasm, but listed below are a few techniques that can guarantee she will have a mind-blowing orgasm with you. Women need a lot more stimulation than men to reach that all-important powerful climax: the mental, physical and emotional stimulation all affect how good her orgasm will be. 4 ways to make her enjoy sex immensely every time:

Create a Relaxed Atmosphere

The ambiance is important if you want to have great sex and help your girl to achieve intense orgasms. The key is to make sure that she is completely comfortable and relaxed. Do things that let her know you appreciate spending time with her: compliment her, surprise her with a nice bottle of wine: it's the little things like that which will set the right mood for great sex!

Take it Slowly

Don't rush straight into sex and have it over in five minutes! Tease and excite her by pleasuring her slowly and being really intimate: this will psyche her up for a really intense orgasm! Sexual excitement comes from not knowing what you are going to do to her or when: take your time and stimulate many different areas of her body. If you already know what she likes you stimulating e.g. her breasts, or her neck, tease these areas first and make her wait for the real pleasuring to begin. This will put her in a really sensual mood and her orgasm will be heightened by all the attention you have given her!

Use props

Traditionally body parts like your tongue, your mouth and hands act as "props". Use a wide range of ways to stimulate her before taking her over the edge into a deep, powerful orgasm. You don't even have to limit yourself to using your body parts as aids to the sexual experience: you can always use food, or other objects to make the sex far more sensuous and the orgasm more powerful. Experimentation can make the sex really exciting and impromptu, and a lot of excitement can be had from not knowing what's going to happen next! It'll stop sex from getting boring and keep her orgasms powerful!

Make her Endure a lot of Pleasure Before Allowing her to Climax

The art of endurance during sex is really sensuous. Holding back in order to increase pleasure to the maximum is a sure-fire way to get her to have an explosive orgasm. Pleasuring her intensely, until she orgasms, is paramount (no getting lazy and slowing down halfway through!). To do this, you can learn how to hold your ejaculation, or tantric sex techniques to prolong her pleasure and make her anticipate the pleasure that is coming next. Tip: If she orgasms before you, you will be able to induce multiple orgasms from her, when you finally ejaculate!

Sexual Healing and Tantra

The term "healing" conjures up images of fixing something that is viewed as broken or unhealthy. Sexual healing would be needed to heal a physical illness or to correct the behavior that is sexually dysfunctional or deviant. Pedophilia, sex addiction, impotence, and frigidity are some examples of conditions for which sexual healing through the aid of a medical or mental health professional would be most appropriate.

Tantra is not a method of sexual healing so much as it is a useful tool for bringing about a change of negative or uncomfortable attitudes towards sexuality and becoming more open, relaxed and sexually whole. Tantric practices, among many other things, help to dispel the most common myths and misconceptions about sexuality to establish an intelligent, rational setting for a natural, healthy, more enjoyable sex life. Tantric practices are useful in enhancing sensitivity to simple sensual pleasures, realigning unbalanced energies, and liberating us from unhealthy cultural beliefs regarding sex and sexual pleasure.

Sensual Enhancement

A major part of tantric practice is to pay close attention to what we see, hear, smell, feel, and taste without analysis or judgment. The more focused attention given to the senses and sensual stimuli, the more sensitive they become, and it takes less to arouse them. Because sex is a highly sensual activity, the enhancement of all sensual perceptions has a direct positive effect on libido and the ability to sustain sexual excitement. More pleasure is enjoyed by less and less effort and without overindulgence. Tantra helps to take us back to a time when a simple touch brought a rush of warm feelings of joy and ecstasy, and this way, the pleasure of touch is greatly extended far beyond the mere moment of physical orgasm.

Energy Balance

Within every one of us are differing energies. Among them are Shiva, the masculine, calm and dynamic; and Shakti, the feminine, earthy, creative, and intuitive. When these internal polarities are balanced and integrated, we are able to take full advantage of the qualities of both such as clarity and intuitiveness, peace, and power. The result is a dynamic whole, the interplay of yin and yang, each capable of giving and receiving (sharing equally) pleasure with a partner. Encounters with others, both sexual and nonsexual feel more egalitarian when there is a lack of competition and constant worry and fear about unfair advantage. Fear and worry block the flow of energies, particular the energies needed for relaxation and fulfillment. Tantric relationships generally promote more cooperation and freedom to experience the joys of sexual playfulness.

Sex and sexuality are but a very small part of Tantra. However, almost all exposure to tantra by westerners derives from misrepresentations and misunderstandings of the practice through some well-meaning so-called healers and some not so well-meaning profiteers. Most often they make easy money by claiming that tantra is limited to sacred sex and a neurotic quest to live out bodily passions. This hyperbolic emphasis on sex positions, prolonged orgasms, sexual healing, controlling ejaculation, etc. simply preys upon the western aversion to sexuality, the unhealthy western fascination with sex and everything sexy, or both and has very little to do with authentic Tantra. Tantra is actually a very simple, deep, subtle spiritual practice in which adherents learn to use sensuality, creative energies, and breath to become completely present to reality, with an open heart, in order to simultaneously experience a greatly expanded state of love-based consciousness.

Chapter 2-   What Is Tantric Sex?

History of Tantra

There is some indefinite quality with respect to the birthplace of the idea of tantric sex, however it is a prevalent view that a network, alluded to as the "Lemurian" individuals were viewed as the primary individuals to rehearse this specific type of holy sex. They thought about the human body as an awesome vessel and used different animating procedures for connecting with the senses so as to bring in spiritual liberation. A few people will, in general, accept that Tantra is identified with the old Indian act of "yoga" too, since these two systems use distinctive substantial stances for shaping a bond with the Cosmos.

Tantric sex has increased a great deal of prevalence in the ongoing past and it has gotten well known in the western world with a ton of famous people like Sting, Madonna and even the late Steve Jobs who had confessed to having attempted this system. Presently, it has gradually discovered acknowledgment everywhere throughout the world. A few idealists do have faith in its viability in accomplishing more noteworthy delight.

Tantric sex fulfills individuals genuinely, intellectually and deeply too. Tantric sex gives total fulfillment and causes the whole body to feel incredibly pleasurable, helps in sincerely interfacing with one's partner and on a deep level; it helps in the amalgamation of two spirits and carries them closer to godliness.

Tantra uses two energies; the female and the male energies. The female energy is alluded to as Shakti, and the male energy is known as Shiva. Shakti and Shiva are Hindu divine beings, and their object of worship revere includes the venerating of Ling and Yon. Linga implies the penis and far off methods the vagina. When a couple participates in tantric sex, then the female energy present in the body, Shakti, ascends through the diverse chakras, and it penetrates through the female community that is alluded to as the Kundalini and afterward it converges with the male energy, alluded to as Shiva. This combination of energies helps in framing a bond that outperforms the human domain.

Tantric Sex or Neotantra is essentially spiritual sex. It takes the old beliefs and teachings of Tantra and brings them into our modern relationships, and sex lives in order to help us better connect in our romantic relationships and to be one with our bodies and sensations. Tantric Sex is about an exchange of energy between partners and getting in touch with the feelings of our body. It is also about removing distractions and being mindful in order to have more intense, longer-lasting, full-body orgasms.

In Neotantric Sex, it is believed that women are generally taught to always focus on the needs of others and taking care of others and to place more importance on the pleasure of others than on themselves. It is believed that women are so disconnected from their feelings and sensations that they must begin a practice of mindfulness in order to reconnect with this part of themselves. It, therefore, teaches women to be more present in their pleasure and, as a result, their orgasms. It is also believed that men generally have short and intense orgasms and that it is possible for them to have better and longer orgasms through practice as well. Neo-tantra focuses on teaching men to be able to prolong their orgasms and make them more all-encompassing and extend their pleasure overall.

Pros and Cons of Tantric Sex

Tantric sex can allow a couple to connect on a much deeper level when having sex than they might otherwise have been able to. This is very beneficial in a marriage or a long-term relationship where the passion has faded.

Pros

Tantric sex can give people new ways of reaching orgasm and can lead both women and men to achieve the greatest orgasms of their lives.

Tantric sex gives insight into why many women have trouble reaching orgasm and how to overcome these challenges.

Cons

Practicing tantric sex and getting good at it takes time and effort on a continued basis, it does not result in an overnight improvement.

It may seem "too spiritual" to those who do not consider themselves to be spiritual beings, or who tend to reject religion.

It may be challenging to connect to your body in this new way, and you may become discouraged by the time and effort it takes to try to accomplish this.

Different Parts Of Tantric Sex

There are three significant primary parts of Tantric sex, and these are tantric correspondence, tantric positions and tantric working out. Tantric correspondence is a procedure that helps in the converging of a couple genuinely and intellectually. This aids in bringing them near each other and is fit for transforming a standard couple into perfect partners.

Tantric positions are sure places that will help in uniting a couple explicitly. There are distinctive tantric activities just as breathing strategies that will help in harvesting the most out of tantric sex. More data about these three parts of Tantric sex has been clarified in the coming.

Tantric sex helps in liberating the body, brain and soul. This is conceivable through the act of the systems as referenced. Quieting one's psyche is a vital part of any training that includes meditation. So also, for practicing tantric sex, it is basic to facilitate your brain. These procedures have been referenced.

In contrast to normal sex, the lessons of tantric sex focus on making the members mindful of their activities while engaged with a sexual demonstration with their partner. If you are aware of your activities, then you can guarantee that you can initiate a sentiment of veneration and even regard for your partner. It is tied in with respecting your body and that of your partner's also. The essential goal of tantric sex is to assist you with loosening up your body and brain. When you can discover this discharge, you will have the option to communicate without any difficulty that will develop and reinforce the security that exists among you and your partner; the sort of love that would bind together your spirits.

Tantric Sex Encourages Your Healing

Maybe one of the best potential employments of tantric sex is that it can help in healing your body and soul. It will likewise assist you with letting go of undesirable thoughts and cause your psyche to feel lighter. You may have been harmed before or might have persevered through some type of dismissal in your past connections. Tantric sex will help you in excusing yourself and will assist you with learning to adore yourself by and by and to appreciate your body as you were intended to. Various strategies have been referenced right now will help you in mending and liberating yourself from any blame or injury that you may have persevered. You will see that you will feel progressively engaged if you follow the guidance that has been given right now. Tantric sex will without a doubt, assist you with mending and it is done through the next advances. You should distinguish the occurrence that has harmed you. This hurt could have been genuine or nonexistent. In this way, the subsequent stage is to decide if it was genuine or fanciful. Sexual incitement will help you in recognizing the distinction. You will have the option to locate the negative feelings connected to this specific damage and can release them. Replace these negative sentiments with positive feelings and encounters that will enable you to heal.

So, what is tantric sex at its core? It's pretty in-depth, and here, we'll talk all about what tantric sex is, the concepts behind it, and why it matters.

Tantric Sex at the Core

Tantric sex is a type of sexual experience that involves more of slowing down, enjoying what you're doing, and feeling the fun and experience of the moment. It's not quick sex, but more slow, methodical, and fun to experience.

The idea behind it is that it's the opposite of a quickie, rushed sex, or anything that seems almost quick and meaningless. This is all about enjoying the other person, and in general, involves increasing intimacy.

An older Practice

This type of sex isn't just some generic type of sex that you have, but instead, it's a methodical, older process that's important to do. It's an ancient Hindu activity that's been occurring for at least five millennia. So yes, this has been around for a little bit.

The concept behind it is that it's the waving and expansion of different energies, bringing them together in a deep, intimate connection with another being.

It is very slow, and the goal of it is to create a connection between the body and mind. This connection is said to bring about powerful orgasms as a result of it.

Chapter 3- Understanding What Tantric Philosophy Is

So, what's the philosophy behind tantric sex? It's quite interesting and very important to know. The philosophy behind this is simple to understand, and very effective to learn.

The Purpose of It

Tantric sex has at a core a purpose that can help you improve your sex life. For most people, there are many goals and expectations that involve how we look at sex, and the way it should be done, along with habits and routines we must follow that make us feel like we're in a rut sexually.

Tantra is about taking all of that and throwing it out the window, so your ultimate goal is to not focus on the routines and habits of sex, but instead starting with a fresh and new look to it. This basically takes out the whole veteran aspects of it, assuming you know everything, and it lets you look at things almost like a beginner.

This refines sex in another way too. It makes it more about connection, intimacy, and the possibility of it that's playful and fun, rather than just racing to have an orgasm.

For most people, tantric sex has as one of the philosophies to learn and rediscover all of this for yourself. Let go of the concept where you have to just "get someone off" or achieve really anything. Once you do that, there's more room for discovery and a lot more fun.

You take out the whole thought process behind this, and instead, look at things in a personalized manner so you can benefit from it too.

Less About The Thoughts, More About The Moments

When we do things, we oftentimes are thinking only about the thoughts, rather than the moments we need to experience. That's why most of us struggle with orgasms because we're so hung up on trying to orgasm that sometimes we don't, or if we do, it's not that memorable or powerful.

But, with tantric sex, you're experiencing everything at the moment, including orgasms that are much more powerful, longer-lasting, a lot more non-ejaculatory, and also the full-body orgasms for both men and women.

That's because, it's less just about the genitalia orgasm, and more about the well, everything else orgasm.

The orgasms that you have are different. They are more about in the moment, where you're not focusing on the mechanics of life, but just well, what you're doing.

It brings a sort of oneness with life, and your partner, something that the Hindu religions try to go for.

While you're not trying to go for nirvana-like in Buddhism, but when you orgasm in a tantric manner, it basically lets you surrender your body, the states of vision, and promotes a oneness between you and the other person.

It's a very spiritual activity, and even those who are reacting it just in a secular manner do experience a glimpse of the divinity because of the melting of your regular self during those moments. When you experience this, it's almost like you're becoming a new, refined person, and in many cases, lets you push through the bad, and experience the good.

For most people in this day and age, we all focus on just the action itself, getting it done so we can go about our business. But, does that really build a connection? Are you really focused on your partner? This is what you have to realize happens with tantric sex.

If you are looking for a good way to compare this, a quickie is literally like a takeout food, whereas tantric sex is a five-star meal that you eat in the restraint. With this type of sex, you're not spending as much time just getting it done just to get it done, but it's slow, savoring, and wonderful to experience, and in turn, is a delicious and mesmerizing experience.

This can also bring some space back into your love life. Do you sometimes think you're just having sex just to have sex? Do you sometimes feel like you're not really engaged in the act of sex? Well, that's the problem. For most people, sex is just a quick and dirty thing, rather than an intimate, wholesome action between two parties. That in turn, will cause your relationship to feel hollow, boring, and not worth it.

But, with tantric sex, you can change the way it all feels. Instead of just taking things like an activity and not really putting more emphasis on it than that, tantric sex involves the action of sex, the doingness of it, but also the connection shared between you and the other being you're with.

It's deeper, more thoughtful for both parties, and a ton of fun.

Why Try Tantric sex?

There is a reasoning behind trying tantric sex. Tantric sex for one, ash been around for thousands of years. It must work pretty well if you're looking to do something different, and have a deeper, more thoughtful connection with another person.

But, if you want to extend the effort and time into sex, you'll start to get a much more intense ecstasy from it.

Which means a much more intense orgasm.

It does work, and there are even celebrities that will do his with their partners, and it's part of the reason why some people will stay together with one another.

And sometimes, it builds that deep, intimate connection with that person that you want. If you feel like your relationship with your partner is a little stale and boring, this is one of the easiest always to spice things up.

If you're sick of doing the same old, same old in bed, then tantric sex is for you. If you want to become more intimate with the person you love, this is for you. If you would like to reconnect with the one that you love, especially after raising kids, or a stressful day, this is for you.

In the hustle and bustle of our world, we might not think that we have time for this type of sex, but it's a great form of sex, and it can change your life, and the lives of others too.

The concept behind this is where you start to realize that all experience that you have, including sexual intercourse, is a personal thing, and has the potential to transform your ability to understand yourself. Everything in life does this, not just having sex, but we're going to talk about the sexual aspects of this in there.

The idea behind this as well is to be aware and enlightened. You're more aware when you're experiencing tantric sex than you would be if you're just having a quickie with your partner. Perhaps you haven't really looked at your partner all that much recently, or maybe you haven't really thought about anything besides everything you want to do after sex.

Well, tantric sex lets you achieve that awareness of the other person, and it's pretty interesting.

While it does have roots in ancient tantra, it's wonderful for those who want to experience a deeper and more immersive sexual experience.

And what's more, is that tantric sex doesn't involve being spiritual at all. You don't have to be a Hindu to participate in tantric sex, but you can apply these principles in order to have a better life and learn about it as well.

Everything you do during tantric sex is a connection. Whether you both synchronize your breathing together, look a one another, or even touch one another while having intercourse. Unlike other types of sex, it isn't a quick and dirty activity, but instead helps prolong the experience with your partner, and deepen the connection with one another.

So now that you know at the core what tantric sex is and the benefits of tantric sex, which we'll talk about.

Chapter 4-   The Benefits Of Tantric Sex

Tantric sex has a myriad of different benefits, and here, we'll highlight and in detail some of the benefits tantric sex has to offer.

Rejuvenates your Sexual Health

Tantric sex is wonderful for sexual health, especially for women, but men do as well.

When you have a lot of orgasms frequently in your brain, it stimulates brain waves, and the chemistry that you have will alter as well.

For many people, sex is used as a way to relax, but it's more than just a simple ejaculation or climax. It's a way to help release those energies which are tied up.

Think about your current sexual health. Do you orgasm a lot? do you sometimes have sex without being fully aroused, or even an orgasm? Sometimes this happens, especially with women. Some women take much longer to get aroused or to even experience orgasms, which means that for them, sex is more than an activity they do to benefit their partner rather than themselves.

But, when you use tantric sex, the idea is to benefit both parties, not just the guy who is having sex, but the woman as well. That means, you'll both have amazing orgasms, and you'll feel better about sex as well. You'll want to have sex more, and sex will be better, more meaningful for you.

That can do a number of great things on both your physical and mental health and we'll that here.

Depression and Stress Relief

Depression and stress are two of the biggest mental hurdles that we have in our world today. However, sex is a way to help relieve it. But, if you're just having quickie after quickie, without really having a deeper, more immersive connection with your partner, can you really say that it's stress-relieving?

Chances are, it's not. You need to have that long, relaxing sexual experience to be happier. While five hours might be excessive, for some people, that's significantly more than the five minutes they were having beforehand.

Tantric sex helps with stress and depression, and it can help you feel better too. When you orgasm, a lot of the stress you experience while having sex magically melts away, resulting in you being happier, and much healthier too.

It can even affect the brain chemistry too, probably in ways you've already experienced, but they're worth mentioning regardless, for example, the endocrine glands start to increase, meaning a much higher high, some serotonin excreted, some DHEA, and testosterone too, which will affect your physical wellness too. All of this is there, and there are even some studies that say when you have more orgasms, you'll experience greater mental health and wellness.

Sex isn't just a temporary orgasm and temporary happiness either. With tantric sex, it takes it to the next level, ups the ante a little bit. When you experience tantric sex, you're experiencing a more intimate and personal connection with the person you love, and that in turn can make you feel utterly amazing.

Tantric sex is a good thing to have, and it's something that, with the way things are sometimes, can really help you mentally feel good.

Depends on the Bond

How many times do you have sex with your partner, and it feels almost…forgettable? Sex shouldn't be some forgettable experience. Some of us have sex for the sake of our partners, and sometimes, we just have sex in order to have sex.

But, with tantric sex, it changes the game. With tantric sex, you're using that connection you've got with the other person, and in turn, building more understanding with the other person, and some wellness and happiness too. You will feel more in-tune with your partner, and much happier as well you'll feel the connection grow between the two of you.

And it isn't just a physical connection, it's a mental connection too. If you sometimes feel the distance between you and your partner, having tantric sex will help you with enjoying the moment, enjoying your partner, and making things better between the two of you as well. So yes, it will help develop a healthier connection and a deeper understanding.

Physical benefits

Orgasms do possess a physical benefit too. They can improve your health a lot, and it can help with making your body stronger too through cardiovascular health, endocrine, and immune function, along with nervous system health too. If you have tantric sex at least twice a week, it releases an antibody that's called immunoglobulin A, or also called IgA, which protects your body from illness.

Orgasms also can help alleviate depression, and help you feel and look younger. Some also believe it'll make your lifespan stronger, strengthening your immune system, and improving the overall health of you too. However, there are still studies that need to be done to completely verify these results.

But, sexual experience and exposure to semen do help boost the moods I most women, and in many cases, it can help with your mood enhancements, your emotional bands, and ultimate intimacy too.

Men and women both can benefit from this too. This isn't just one or the other, but having sex together will provide these benefits since it'll be an activity both of you participate in too.

There is also the fact that it can be a wonderful cardio for the body. Sex burns a lot of calories, and orgasm does too. That's why, it's imperative you consider this since even making love requires energy, and if you're going for a long time, it can be a wonderful workout.

It also naturally relaxes the body. Tantric sex, in particular, does it, since you're calming both the body and the mind down in order to be in-sync with your partner. That mutual togetherness alone stimulates your vagus nerve, thereby relaxing the body and promoting wellness too. Over time, you'll start to feel the muscles that were stretched start to relax, and you'll practice diaphragmic breathing too.

Tantric sex is great for the physical body, and it is a good thing to do for you, not just because it feels great, but because it makes you feel great too.

Chapter 5- A Woman's Orgasm

Tantric sex, in particular, will help with a woman's orgasm. There is a big difference between the ordinary orgasm that you get from sex and tantric orgasms, and oftentimes, it will change how the woman feels.

Many times, these can last for hours, and in women, this can change their sexual health. There is a command during a tantric orgasm that reaches your brains' control center, and hat's through the hypothalamus and the pituitary gland, and I will majorly benefit the sex life of women in particular.

A lot of the hormone oxytocin gets released during a tantric orgasm, and this alone can boost your mood, the position you feel in life, your passion, your emotion, and your social skills. Having tantric sex can do all of this, and I can benefit you in your daily activities.

It'll Make You More Patient

Tantric sex isn't just for sexual pleasure, it helps with developing life skills and building on weaknesses.

Do you sometimes kind of just want to get it done rather than go through the deep connection w=in the moment? You might not even realize it because your body and mind are fueled by hormones, but tantric sex promotes patience, which is something of a virtue that everyone can have during sex. However, this can also help you to build a deeper, better connection with your partner.

Sometimes, tantric sex is a little bit awkward, since many people aren't used to just sitting there, focusing on their partner, breathing together, and developing a real look at the person they're with. Some people don' even realize they do this either.

Do you tend to have sex with either your eyes closed or the lights off? While dimming the lights aids to the ambiance, tantric sex makes it a little different. Tantric sex is actually a meditative process, and they encourage you to hold back the orgasm. It didn't denial, it's your conscious effort to hold it back so you and your partner can have a conscious moment together.

Patience develops naturally from this. You might not even realize it, but you learn to understand and appreciate your partner a whole lot more after engaging in tantric sex. Those things that used to piss you off every now and then? Well now, if you practice tantric sex, this patience develops, and you grow stranger with your partner over time.

Helps with Problem Solving

This might seem a bit strange, but for those starting, it's a different type of activity that you might not be used to. Those who are beginners or new to the experience might realize that the positions required for tantric sex are much more varied than just the same old positions.

Some of them might not even provide much pleasure to you either.

This requires you to work together with your partner. It has sex a team activity, where both of you need to talk it out and work together as well, in order to enjoy pleasure.

This can oftentimes be embarrassing because both of you are vulnerable in this state, but it helps with problem-solving skills and builds that connection. Plus, if you're a team, you'll have a much stronger connection outside of the bedroom, and work to solve the problems you have going on outside of the bedroom as well.

This also stimulates creativity. That's because we're embracing the concept of "supra sexuality" which expresses our purpose which is creativity and empowerment in order to unlock our full potential. Sex might be used to create human life of course, but it also brings forth new and creative actions that will help you experience a pleasurable sensation in order to achieve the goals that you have during intercourse as well.

Let's You Be Selfless

Do you sometimes feel like your partner is a little selfish in the bedroom? Do you sometimes feel you might be a tiny bit selfish? It might be because of the fact that you're not withholding your orgasm.

There is a benefit to doing this, and that's something to mention. Oftentimes, people don't realize that tantric sex offers the power of liberation, which allows for you to have an amazing experience that is often compared to glimpsing into the cosmic consciousness of the other person, fostering a deeper, more responsible understanding of the person.

Oftentimes, some people don't realize how selfish they are until they have the tantric orgasm, which will change their life and blow their minds. Oftentimes, they might not even realize that they are like this until it happens.

But for the other person, it can benefit them too. Sex is a two-person activity, and if you and your partner are both not talking out what will benefit the other person, and your partner isn't being a little bit selfless, it can cause problems later on. You need to walk into this with the idea of supporting one another into orgasms, since this will help others remember and get a better idea of giving, rather than just receiving.

We're a culture focused on the receiving end of sex. While it's fun, also giving to the other person can have some marked benefit to you as well.

Creates More Empowerment

Finally, it'll make you feel empowered.

What does empower actually mean? It's more than just mere power. Power is something that most people confuse empowerment with, but they're very different.

The organic sexual pleasure that you get from tantric sex strips away the pretenses and helps check your ego. Empowerment is what comes after you check your ego, and experience the wild nuances of tantric sex. It oftentimes brings about that vulnerability, stripping away all of the other stuff that you might've hidden or been ashamed off, giving you a sense of purpose, and the ability to express your fears and loves on a deeper level.

For those of us who have trouble being this vulnerable, this can be scary. I get that, but understand that, with the right mindset, and the right understanding of the fact that you're in this for the long haul, and you'll experience pure, unadulterated pleasure, is something amazing.

You'll realize over time that you're stronger, and you can tackle on more of life. People who experience tantric sex have power, but it isn't a power that they use for bad or a power that they don't know how to wield. Now, it's their own sense of power they've learned from experiencing this, which is mind-blowing.

People don't realize how this changes you, how having tantric sex will blow your mind, but also, strip you of all of the facades you've put up about sex. The idea of hiding under the sheets, turning the lights off, not looking at your partner, all of that gets fully stripped away through tantric sex.

Chapter 6-   How Best To Prepare Your Mind And Body For Tantric Sex Using Techniques For Foreplay, Massage, And Masturbation

Talk To Your Partner

Before you begin with this, always make sure that you and your partner both want to try this. Remember, it takes two to tango, and that goes for tantric sex especially. If you're interested in doing it, you need to make sure that your partner is on the same page as you are. Most people don't realize that this is something that your partner may not be ready for.

While you think starting right away is a great idea, but here's the thing: you have to, with tantric sex, this since it is a two-part procedure and something that you'll have to do together. If you're both not interested or working together, it won't happen.

Plus, if you're practicing tantric sex but they're not, it would mean only one of you is going to experience powerful orgasms and want to take it slower, while the other will be doing the opposite. It seems a little bit unfair, right? That's the main issue you run into with tantric sex if you experience it any other way, it's that you're not going to make it work, and you won't really get the results.

And it shouldn't be hard to convince your partner to try it. After all, you want deeper intimacy between you and the other person, better sex, more passion, and just more fun between the two of you.

This is simple to get your partner's agreement on since it is probably something, they'll enjoy from the spicing up and variety alone.

Prepare The Body

Preparing the body is a good thing to do with tantric sex because it takes time. Oftentimes, people don't realize that tantric evenings can be a bit physically demanding. It oftentimes also makes you feel better about yourself too. You'll appreciate the way your body feels, and the wellness you experience.

When you feel good physically and the room is arranged how it should be, it'll tranquilize you, making lovemaking some of the best there is.

So what are some things that you can do? Well first and foremost, if you're not someone who wants to spend hours at the gym, or work too hard on their physical fitness, then try yoga.

Yoga is one of the best choices that you'll experience. It is a great thing that will help with improving your experience.

Not only that, yoga helps with flexibility, and there are postures that will change your sex life too. Some of them can even be used during tantric sex. Plus, it helps with realigning the energy.

It's deduced that energies you have flowed from your spine, so you should always make sure that you have a relaxed back that isn't hunched over. You should also do this n a way where you're not hurting yourself, and it isn't physically affecting the back.

Diet Tips

Diet is the next area to focus on. Diet is actually on par with physical fitness, but for tantric nights it also helps improve them. Diet doesn't mean you have to follow a complex menu that some guru put together, but what you should do is eat in a manner that's healthier than ever. The best way to do it is to have habits that are healthy, and you practice moderation. Try to abstain from overindulging as you get closer and closer to the tantric night. You should try to not eat a lot of heavier foods right before having tantric sex, and also don't overconsume alcohol either.

You should stay hydrated, but also not drink a ton of water too much once you get closer to time. That's because you want to keep things steamy, and while bathroom breaks happen, you don't want that hindering everything.

Also, look for safe detox recipes, with the focus being on safe. You should look for ones that have happy users, and those who have some complaints so you could also look at the difference between them.

But you should also look at safety concerns too. If you have a condition that's also affecting your ability to do a diet, also research the side effects of that.

You should also try to snack minimally, and if you do snack, you should also be mindful of what you're eating. There's a lot that you can eat that's healthy and good for you, and a lot that you should minimize. Go through and look for all of these, so you can better understand what you're doing, and also don't overindulge in these as well. Because let's face it, do you really need to gorge on those cookies? Probably not.

Relaxing The Body

Before you get into tantric sex, you should try to relax the body. Relaxing the body is very important because if you're not relaxed, you're going to feel a bit exhausted, and probably sick from the stress. After a bad day, even if you didn't do a whole lot, it'll feel like you've fought with a bear and lost.

The body is important to relax, but you should also make sure that you relax the mind to. Mental stress does weaken your immune system, and bacteria and viruses love when that happens.

Learning to relax is a possible thing, but the big thing to remember here is to not float around like you're in a Zen haze. You might live in a chronic-stress situation though, and that becomes the new normal for many. Lots of times, people don't realize how stressed out they are, and the debts, demands, and coping skills oftentimes are a reason why people drift apart. This is a big thing to understand because tantra helps you build a bond that's closer than ever before, that's more than just sex for many people.

Oftentimes, relaxing is a hard-pressed concept. You probably might have issues with a long-term stress reliever, but a nap, a shower, or a movie that's funny is definitely helpful. Meditation is valuable, but it's an overlooked thing, but you need to learn to accept that you're stressed out, and you need to spend time preparing yourself for this. If you're a bit sad about the way that you look, try to maybe spend 30 minutes a day walking or working out. It does bring about liberation to you in its own way. Plus, if you're relaxed, you'll practice tantra way better, and accept all of this in the long run.

What to Wear

Some people think that you need to wear very tight and sexy clothes. No, wear something that's loose, comfortable, and you should try to put something on that makes you feel good. Some people will dress in attire that reflects certain deities or the east. But it can help bring about the art of tantra into the bedroom

However, you should also focus on being clean and happy with yourself before you practice tantra.

First, brush your teeth and hair prior to what you do. This is a quick and simple thing to really bolster your confidence and make it easier for you to do as well.

Some people like to do a ritual bath beforehand, but that is something that you don't have to do. You should make sure that it's a bit structured, and that you have the aim of making sure that you are bonded, but not bonded enough to have sex yet. You should wash one another in ways that are on-sexual and use soaps and oils that are scented. This fosters anticipation between the two people, and it's something that you'll enjoy with the other person.

You should do things together that foster anticipation between both of you as well. That will, in turn, benefit both of you, and it does bring about an honorable and artful experience with your partner.

Setting Your Scene

You should set the scene up by putting rituals into sex, and make sure that your space is set up. Most people focus on making sure there's a lot of white in the room, such as in the form of pillows, candles, and also soft music. You should do this with the intent of making the sex feel special.

For most people, they just rush into the bedroom and don't really work to set the mood. But, if you really want to make it memorable for both parties, you should try decorating it. Soft, sensual music will help bring forth a better, more intimate experience between both of you. Music is great for sex period, but soft, sensual music will change the way sex is for both parties and brings forth a sense of understanding, wellness, and happiness as well.

Breathe Away!

Before you even start, you should breathe and make sure that you do it in a way that benefits you. This is a good way to mentally calm yourself down, and to help you relax. What you should do, is take one full breath in through the nose, fill the belly with air, and then exhale. You should notice your belly move outwards. That's your diaphragm breathing, and you should make sure that you do focus on getting that type of breathing. When you exhale, you should see the belly start to return to normal size.

If you're having issues with this, you should visualize that pushing the pelvis down through there, and you push the breath directly to the floor. Try to do this a few times before you do it during sex so it becomes more automatic so that you can really benefit from this too.

Try Massages

Finally, before you have sex, you should try massaging. These massages don't have to be a long time, but you should try to switch off between the giver, and the receiver of leisure. You might ask your partner to rub your feet for a couple of minutes, and then do whatever they like for a couple of minutes.

During each turn, don't be afraid to give the feedback that you need to. It's okay to tell your partner what it is they should do better, and this will help them really give you what you want.

This is something most couples struggle with. By talking to the other person, you will be able to really get what you want. Communication is something that most people need to understand has to be there. The way you work together is a great way for you to learn. You will be able to teach your lover what you want, and they'll teach you what they want, creating the best sexual experience possible for you.

You should pay attention to the way their hands feel, the way they touch you, the sensual nature of this, and from there, relax the body and the mind. This will help you improve your ability to handle this, and make it so that you're happier and better than ever.

Chapter 7- Sexual Personality

There is no denying that a man with a sexual personality is like a precious gem for women. The whole thing, of course, is that women badly seek a sexual man in their lives. They feel excited and fulfilled when they surrender their sexuality and emotions in front of a sexual masculine man. They have always known it that a man with sexual personality can make their dream future come true. That's why; women always keep the exclusive attitude, unconsciously, for finding their fantasy man.

Superstars and Leaders vs. Average Men

It does not matter whether you have got an exclusive lady (soul-mate) or dating with different girls. But if you do not have sexual personality, you will murder your attraction brutally very soon. Also, it is very important to clear you that body language is not the only thing that makes you extremely attractive. It definitely helps you in projecting yourself as a confident man but it does not curl the toes of women with sexual attraction. There are maybe numerous tips on attraction but still movie directors, especially, are protecting some hidden traits of their heroes. They turn their ordinary hero into an extraordinary sexual personality and make women lust after him wildly.

Let's take a moment now and notice how a superstar turns himself into the fantasy man of women. Well, there are literally hundreds of hidden traits which he uses to highly attract women. And no, he does not use the power of his fame or money and you know that every girl would love to marry even with a poor superstar. Actually, you are using certain games in attraction about which every girl knows. On the other hand, superstars dominate the mind of women with their hidden traits and sexual personality. Here, an example that will make you understand the difference between attraction and extreme sexual attraction.

Average confident man: "He will use his body language and pick up lines for getting the girls' attention."

Superstar: "A superstar will notice her and keep the eye contact from across the room, forgetting her attention." (This is what makes women melt)

A woman loves to connect with a man through some story. She highly loves to tell her friends that their eye met across the room, instead, he used to pick up line on me. So, this is what makes a superstar get girls in bed within the first several hours of meeting.

Sexual Personality Tips

For having sexual personality, there is not about faking anything. Research shows that if we want a remarkable change in our personality then we need to focus on the smallest hidden things. Men who utilize the power of the smallest hidden elements of attraction always spread their sexual charm on women.

Sexual Movements: Your body always screams out the truth. There are thousands of tips on confident body language. Moreover, these tips are not only necessary but also common among men. Unfortunately, those default tips project you as a confident man, for the time being, but never make you sexual.

Walk With Big Slow Steps

Women can judge a man's sexuality by only noticing the way he walks. If you hold yourself in a confident manner but walk with short fast steps, she will instantly get that you are not naturally confident. That's why; you need to walk with big calm steps because that's what makes you sexual.

Have you ever noticed wrestlers? They walk with big slow steps and while standing, they keep at least one-foot distance between their feet. The ways they walk and stand make them sexual lion for women. Also, they exist in women's naughty and sexual fantasies.

Small Bites

They are hundreds of guys who enjoy huge bites on their dates. It does not matter whether you are with your friends or date. Your huge bites will present you funny, not sexual. Now, here is the interesting part, a man with small bites always gets noticed instantly by women. Your bites make women discover your true sexual nature. So, always prefer small bites instead of huge bites.

Your little details are always much important than you believe. Now, you can understand why most of the guys never get their second dates or why they fail to keep their wives attracted towards them. Your small details make women notice your sexual personality. Below are a few tips that will make women see you as their sexual fantasy man. These below things are extremely attractive for women.

Keep an exclusive woman in your hands. That exclusive woman can be your friend or secretary. First, this move will keep your values high in front of people, especially women. Second, an exclusive woman in your hands not only helps you in your business but also brings lots of other women into your arena.

A tough guy is far sexual than a bad boy.

After projecting your sexual personality, you always need to strike first because she is desperately waiting for you.

Speak through your chest, instead of the neck. This will make your tone manly and sexy.

Always do slightly overdressing. Use uppers, coats, and jackets. A man with slightly overdressing is sexual for women. Also, use dress-shirts instead of shirts. Your grown-up clothing matters to women.

For having sexual personality, you have to be a man, not a boy. Use attache case, wrist watch, and coat. These things are not only very important for your sexual personality but also earn respect for you.

3 Most Common Woman Sexuality Personalities - Which One Do You Want?

Within today are getting more experienced and more particular in their sexual lives. Most women have had great sex in the past it is important that she continues to experience great sexual performance in order to keep interested. Here are the 3 most common types of women in sex:

The Leader - this could come in the form of a dominatrix or simply a woman who likes to be in control during sex. This could also come in the form of her wanting the man to be the leader. Some women want to be dominated so their man is going to take them and push her to the limits. While other women would like to be in complete control over him by making him beg and worship everything about her body.

You should know which one your woman prefers as long as you pay close attention. If she seems gentle, add a little roughness and see how she responds. If she's being forceful, pay close attention to her body and let her feel like she has total control of the situation.

Exhibitionist - women are normally shy or subsided when showing their bodies. Some women feel it is exciting to be on display somewhere where there is a chance or risk of being caught. Women like this usually must be comfortable with you enough to do it. She may be open to sex outdoors and deep down inside she is not really want to be seen but enjoys the exhilaration.

Role player - if you notice your woman is completely comfortable with themselves and their sexuality it could be a front. This type of women feels more comfortable by pretending to be something or someone else to help them to be freer. You may notice a change in her tone, a change in her personality or more aggressive attitude. Usually, she doesn't one here her name because this may bring her back to reality to lessen the mood.

Regardless of what type of women and her sexual desires that you would like to attract, it is very important that you are able to fully satisfy her. The most common ways to make sure she is fully satisfied is to make sure that your penis size is more than adequate and that you are able to perform long enough for her to climax.

Chapter 8-   Sex Positions

After learning and perfecting on the art of seduction and foreplay, you reach a point where sex is inevitable. While you could have done pretty well in seduction and foreplay, you could disappoint in the actual sexual activity if you lack mastery of various positions. You should engage your partner in an explorative manner as you aim to achieve sexual satisfaction for both of you.

To begin with; you should understand that the classification of sex positions depends on the following formations.

Man on Top face to face

This position is common among partners and is characterized by face-to-face interaction. The standard position of this type is the missionary position where the woman lies back with legs apart. The man lies on top and may use the position for anal or vaginal intercourse. At some point, the woman may dangle her leg on the edge of the platform or lift them towards the ceiling in what is commonly known as the butterfly position. You could practice the same while kneeling. In another variation, the woman may rest the legs on the shoulders of the man. In a coital alignment position, the man points the penis down to make it rub against the clitoris as they make an upward movement. Besides, the woman lies back and raises the legs to the head or put them next to the ears. The man then holds the partner's ankle or instep and lies at the full length of the woman. Most partners prefer this style for it nurtures them emotionally and physically. They can communicate and read body language as they engage in intimacy.

Pros

Eye contact- with this position, the parties can read facial expressions while maintaining eye contact for ultimate pleasure.

Spicing up- With this position, the partner has their hands free and could engage in caressing, kissing, and stimulating the clit.

Dominant man- The position makes the man take full control of the pace, speed, and degree of penetration.

Relaxation- Women prefer this position for they are left relaxed lying on the bed.

Reproduction- Variations of this position are best for reproduction as the man makes a deep penetration which makes him ejaculate near the cervix.

Communication- The position enhanced body language and direct feedback as the partner try new outfits.

Afterthought- The position makes it easier for the man to hold on the woman even after sex by cuddling and kissing her.

Short shafts- It is a solution, especially for any men with a relatively shorter penis. He can control it and avoid slipping out of the vagina.

Cons

Motion- The position has a limited range of motion. The man may be challenged by gravity, preventing him from making a complete stride.

Uncontrolled ejaculation- Men in this position are unable to control their body as they are busy supporting themselves and making strides. For that reason, they are unable to slow their ejaculation.

Incomplete penetration- It is common, especially if the woman is wide around her waist. The thighs might be hindering the man from making a deep penetration.

Less stimulation- Most variations of this position make the woman raise her legs on the man's shoulders or chest. The position makes the penis land downwards, and the clit moves upward leaving them little or no stimulation.

Penetrating from Behind

Most of these styles work for both anal and vaginal sex. The method is sometimes described as the doggy style, although it has numerous variations. In this style, the woman lies and keeps her torso horizontal to allow penetration from behind. Similarly, the torso could be angled downwards while the man raises the hips for thorough penetration. By bending the knees, the penetrating partner could place their feet besides those of their partner and rise as high as possible to maintain penetration.

The man could place the hands on the partner's back to avoid falling forward. The woman could also kneel upright as the man pulls her arms back towards him. Another variation of this style is known as spooning, where partners face the same direction either by kneeling, standing, or lying on the bed.

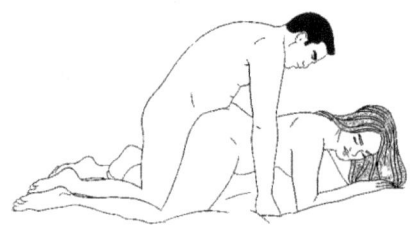

Pros

Free Hands- With this position, both partners can use their hands to make further stimulation with each other.

Ideal Sensation- This is for the men who feel aroused by the smooth sensation of the butt. It creates a pleasurable feeling keeping the couples engaged.

Double Stimulation. As the man enjoys the stimulation from the butt, he could make sexy touches on the clit to share the moment.

Reproduction- The deep penetration associated with this position makes it easy to fertilize your woman as it deposits the sperms near the cervix.

Sound Effects- The soft flesh around the woman's buttocks makes a rhythmic sound to match your thrusts.

Cons

Eye Contact- The fact that the penetration is initiated from behind means no eye contact unless the woman turns. It makes it hard to understand your partner's feelings.

Potential Damage- If men decide to hit hard and miss the vagina, they might injure their penis. Similarly, the position contracts the vagina, making it possible for the man to pound the uterus accidentally.

Woman on Top

This style is for both anal and vaginal penetrations. Other names for it include cowgirl, cowboy, or woman on top. The most characteristic feature of this style is that the man lies on their back as the receiving ones sit or lie on them. The technique allows space for the woman to face opposite direction commonly known as the reverse. They could also squat facing the man leaving only the genitals at contact. On the lateral coital position, the man sits on his back while the receiver rolls slightly sit on him with legs widely apart. This style shares similar features as the missionary only that the woman is on top in this case. By being on top, the woman is less relaxed as compared to the penetrator.

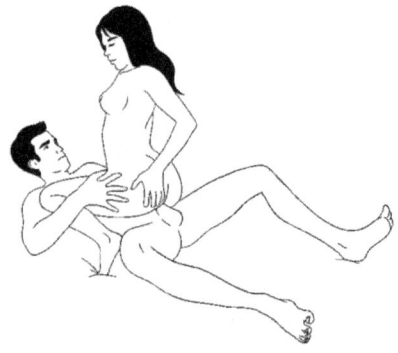

Pros

Eye Contact- Similar to the man on top, the partners can maintain direct eye contact and read the facial expressions.

Hands-On- Partners could use their hands in caressing each other and stimulating the genitals.

Access to Clit- The position puts the man in a perfect position to reach and rub on the clitoris.

Visual Stimulation- Men at this position are also able to see the real thing as it happens, thus arousing their sexual feelings.

Controlled Ejaculation- It is the best position for men who would like to control their ejaculation period. Due to the lack of pressure and effort, a man can control his excitement at times.

Regulated Pace- A woman being on top means that she controls the pace, speed, and depth of penetration.

Pregnancy- Women prefer this position when they are pregnant for it puts less pressure on their belly. Similarly, lactating mothers may use it to control all aspects of intercourse.

Relaxation to Men- As the woman is busy riding on top, the man relaxes under her as long as the penis remains strongly erected. It is an ideal position for men who may be recovering from a sickness.

Cons

Tiresome- Women find this position as tiresome as it leaves them with all the vital responsibilities.

Sliding Out- Men complain that the position allows the penis to slip out, especially if they have a short penis. Similarly, the position might be less favorite for men who have erectile dysfunction. To perfect in this position, you must have and maintain a remarkably strong erection.

Passive Men- For men who believe to be the controllers of the events, this position snatches away the supremacy. It leaves them to watch as the woman takes control of the session. However, they could try raising their hips to participate.

Sitting and Kneeling

Pounding on the spot is the most common style in this category, there is little to describe than what the words describe. The technique generally involves the woman sitting on the man to caress the erogenous zones gently. In a different case, the man could sit on a chair while the receiving one makes a lap dance on him. You could also perform the same in a reverse position where the man faces the back of the woman. The partners could even sit on a couch with armrests. The woman then sits on the partner's laps perpendicularly. For short chairs, the man may kneel while the woman lies on her back putting the ankles on his shoulders. The style works better when you do not have ample space to move around or stretch. Just as an example, you may be on transit and your caravan lacks a restroom making you utilize the space provided on seats. It is also a relaxing style, as both partners are supported. It makes the partners focus on the main activity and move only the parts critical for good sex.

Pros

Reflexes- The position allows the partners to choose between variations and sit or kneel as they engage. The position is a physical feat and a refreshing one too.

Convenient- It can be practiced on a less prepared room or transit. You do not require a raised roof to try it out.

Less Noisy- Due to the closeness of the genitals, the position requires less pressure hence the quietness associated with it.

Placement- In this position, the partners are close together as they may hold each other or face the same direction. This posture ensures that the penis is in the right position as the vagina.

Concentrated Thrusts- The closeness of the position, as well as the genital's placement, enables the man to concentrate on the thrusts.

Interaction- If the partners sit or kneel facing each other, they enhance visual stimulation and can prolong their kisses and caressing.

Cons

Requires a Degree of Physical Fitness- Kneeling for a long time may be troublesome for some couples making the position hard to maintain.

Tiresome- If the woman decides to sit on top of the man; it could prove to be exhausting, especially if she is overweight.

Limited Penetration- This position requires the woman to stretch her feet beyond the man. The feet may hinder the man from making deep impact penetration.

Standing: If you would prefer having sex while standing, then there are numerous variations that you could incorporate. You could engage in vaginal sex while standing facing each other. The woman could allow for penetration by slightly opening up her thighs. In case one of the partners is shorter, they could wear high heels or stand on a stair. The thrusts are more substantial, especially if the woman is leaning on a wall. The position provides support for both partners and could best be applied in upright places such as a shower or bedroom. The standing positions can also work by the woman wrapping her arms around the man's neck and her legs around his waist. This style leaves the vagina and the anus exposed to the erect penis.

Pros

Quickie- The position is the most preferable if you want to do quickie or do not have time to go to the bedroom.

Role Play- The position allows both the man to switch roles as they are both on a similar posture.

Physical Connection- A standing position enhances full-body contact, especially if the couples are completely naked.

Support- When the woman leans on the wall, it provides firm support for both partners. This way, the man could find an opportunity to make a deep penetration.

Caressing- In this position, both partners can hold and kiss, especially if they face each other.

Cons

Shorter Partners- The position might be awkward for partners of different heights. The genitals may not align, requiring one partner to change posture.

Requires Planning- When practicing this position, partners should plan before making moves. It would help them avoids falling off as the man exerts passion, power, and aggression.

Chapter 9- Tantric Sex

What is tantric sex, and how can it improve lovemaking? Tantric sex originated from the tantric practice in Tibetan Buddhism, which began in India. It involves mediation and strengthening one's spirituality. The practice of tantric sex is closely associated with the pattern of mediation and connectivity. It incorporates sexual intimacy to create and enhance a deeper bond and experience with your partner. It is not a casual posture or technique. It requires study, meditation, and practice to achieve the best outcome and benefits.

The Lotus Position

This is a position that requires patience and practice; however, it is rewarding once you get used to it. The lotus involves one partner (usually male) seated on a firm but soft surface, such as a bed or soft rug, with his legs folded (or cross-legged). As he becomes erect, his partner (usually female) will slowly descend onto him, with both feet placed firmly next to him so she can softly land onto him as he slips inside. Once both are fully settled into this position, the woman's arms and legs are wrapped around the man, and he reciprocates with a similar embrace. This is a deeply intimate pose. The couple can look into each other's eyes at close proximity and embrace during the full experience of lovemaking. The woman can slightly lift and adjust within the position to gain a slightly different angle, which can allow her to experience more pleasure and possibly orgasm. To make this a successful pose, use a lot of lubrication and take it slow. This is not a position that accommodates a quick motion or thrust but rather a slower, more tantric pace.

The Butterfly

This position is a fun and ambitious pose that requires a bit of flexibility. In this pose, the man is standing, while the woman is lying on her back with her legs held in the air, though not too far apart, so as to be able to place each one on her partner's shoulders. In doing this, the man can easily penetrate and gently push against his partner's legs as he enters deeper.

This position gives the man a full view of the woman as he penetrates her; he can be standing at the edge of the bed during this process or with legs bent on the bed in the same fashion. For some women, keeping their legs slightly bent makes the transition into this position easier until they become more comfortable.

Three-Legged Dog

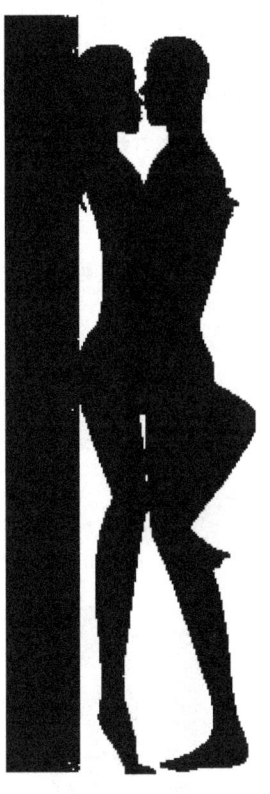

This position is done standing up, usually with one partner against a wall for added support, and one leg raised so that the partner can easily enter and penetrate. It is not the easiest feat to pull off, though it is fun despite the challenge, and can be done in a variety of places. For the woman, having her back against the wall is a good support during this pose. Moreover, lifting one leg can be done with some support; the man holds and positions the lifted leg slightly higher or to the side so that he can enter easily. There is a bit of fine-tuning that involves figuring out at which angle is best to enter. Another variable to consider is the height of both individuals. If one person is taller (the male), it may be easier to enter when the woman is standing on a support or at a higher level. Alternatively, the male can bend or maneuver his position to lower his stance and accommodate a different height. This three-legged dog works easiest for people who are similar in height, though it can be achievable for anyone if you are willing to get creative and flexible (Emery, 2018).

The Hot Seat

This position involves the man sitting in a kneeling position with his upper body leaning back, allowing for his partner, facing in the same direction and knelt in the same fashion, to slip her legs in between his, which are apart enough to enter inside from behind. As she leans back, they become closer, with his arms wrapping around her torso as she reaches for his waist from behind. This position works well in slow, steady motion.

Chapter 10- Advanced Positions

The Head Rush

This position requires the man to move to the edge of the bed with his upper body off of the bed and preferably resting on the floor. The woman then takes her position on top. This position is called the Head Rush because the extended length of time in this position will literally make the man's blood rush to his head, effecting a head rush. This could also refer to the case of blood rushing to both his "heads."

Face Off

This is a very erotic sexual position and is done while sitting on a chair or on the edge of the bed. The woman then sits facing the man and wraps her arms around his back and controls the level of intensity of thrusts by riding up and down the male shaft.

This allows for a lot of intimacy and is a very comfortable position which will allow long drawn-out sex sessions.

This is also called the Lap Dance.

The Hot Seat

This is the reverse of the Lap Dance or Face Off position and can also be done by using either the edge of the bed or a chair. What this basically requires is for the man to sit on the edge of the bed and then allow the woman to sit on his member.

This is also known as The Love Seat and or The Man Chair.

The Pole Position

This is a slight variation of the reverse cowgirl but will require a little bit more effort from the man as he has to keep one leg outstretched in the air. The woman then assumes the position and grabs hold of the outstretched thigh as a means of dual support.

This is also known as the Thighmaster.

The One Up

Every woman's vagina and clitoris is unique. This therefore means that there are varying levels of sensitivity for women. This sexual position is targeted towards women who have particular sensitivity to one side of their clitoris.

This requires having the woman lie on the edge of the bed with one leg raised supported by wrapping her hands around her hamstring just below the knee. This will allow her to have more control of her hip movements and it can assist you in locating the perfect spot to achieve maximum stimulation.

The Spider

This may sound a little bit complicated but is actually very easy to perform. What this will require is a little bit of choreography between you and your partner.

What this requires is for the man to sit on the bed with the woman seated on his lap. The partners face each other with arms back for support. Now here's the complicated part: you will have to move in time with each other thrusting forward, or you can rock back and forth in unison. This position allows for a very erotic view as the woman has her hips between the man's spread legs with her knees bent and feet outside of his hips. Both partners can maintain eye contact while they are performing this sexual act.

This act is also called the Crab Walk.

Getting a Leg Up

This is a slight modification of the Crab Walk. Instead of the woman's legs spread out on the bed, she lifts these up onto the man's shoulders.

This can lead to very quick orgasms as the woman is able to control her pelvic movements easily.

Bottom's Up

Are you up for a bit of a challenge? Well, here's one! The Bottom's up is a little bit difficult to perform as it requires a little bit of contortionism and athleticism. First, the woman lies on her back and the man straddles her as she is facing away. Next, she lifts her legs to wrap them around his back and at the same time to elevate her pelvic region for easy entry. Last, she then grabs on to the man's buttocks and, with a concerted effort, slides up and back.

You'll have to try it to find out just how pleasurable it is!

Sidewinder

The man and the woman lie on their sides facing each other. Spreading her legs, the woman allows for the man to enter her. In this position, the couple can see each other and this encourages a lot of physical contact like hugging and kissing.

This is also called the facing spoon.

The Horny Mantis

This is a variation of the sidewinder. While in the sidewinder position, the female lifts her leg up and over her partner's body and locks him in place by securing her leg on the man's back. This position allows for deeper penetrations.

The Standing Dragon

This move is a modified doggy style where the man has to stand while the woman gets on all fours at the edge of the bed. She will have to spread out a little bit more than usual and arch her buttocks more for this position.

Entering from behind, the man gets a very erotic view of her buttocks as he pounds into the woman. Thrusting in this position can be done lightly or as aggressively as the woman wants.

Another fun name for this is the Crouching Tiger, Hidden Serpent.

The X Position

The X position is basically what its name portrays. It will require you and your partner to lie facing each other with your legs forward and over on top of each other. This forms an X, hence the name.

This position is a bit limiting so thrusting is instead replaced with small gyrations which prolong arousal and lead to great orgasms.

Wheelbarrow, Standing (The Hoover Maneuver)

Everyone knows that sex burns calories but the wheelbarrow has to be credited as one of the sex positions that can really give you a workout!

The man enters the woman from behind and then lifts up her legs and locks these in place by his waist. Now, the couple can stroll around the house while at the same time having sex and burning calories.

Chapter 11- Extra Kama Sutra Positions

The Position of Indrani

Closing out the three recommended positions for High Congress is The Position of Indrani, which is also known as the Position of the Wife of Indra. To get into this pose, the woman will lay on her back and spread her thighs open. She will bend so that her thighs are on the ground on either side of her. Her legs should fold on top of her thighs, with her claves resting on the back of each thigh. This is a very tricky position and requires a high degree of flexibility on the woman's part. If you are unable to master it on your first go, simply bend the thighs back towards the floor as much as possible, and then work towards it over time. Even in the Kama Sutra, it is noted that this is a position that requires much practice, so do not feel discouraged if it does not come naturally to you.

This is the position of the Highest Congress and is the most useful for couples who are experiencing size differences. For larger sized men, this is the best position to assist with penetration, as the woman's vagina is opened up perfectly to allow for insertion. If you are finding the woman is unable to have her legs pushed back enough to make it work, the man should assist her as much as possible, by using his forearms to press down against the back of the woman's thighs. Do note, however, that you should not press down too hard, as you don't want to injure her in the process. Only push as far as she is comfortable, and never force her legs or cause any strain in the process.

The Side Clasping Position

The first of the Low Congress positions, the Side Clasping Position has both the man and woman laying on their side. To begin, the man should lay down on his left side, and the woman will lay on her right side so that she is facing him. Keeping her legs tightly pressed together, and him with his legs tightly together, he should then press himself against the woman's body and enter her from this position. Both the partner's legs should remain in a straight posture for the entire duration, and their bodies should stay tightly pressed against each other. There will be no space for the man to caress the woman's breasts, but he can run his hands along her back and buttocks.

As you may be able to tell immediately, this is a position that makes penetration a bit more difficult. The vagina is closed and hidden between the legs which are tightly pressed together. This is why it is the position of Lowest Congress, as it is designed to be most beneficial for couples where the woman has a larger yoni and the man has a smaller lingam. Surprisingly, however, this position may not actually be as possible for men with smaller penises, as the distance needed to properly penetrate requires more length from the man. We would say that in general, this position is not typically a favorite of most couples, but that doesn't mean it isn't worth trying. If you can accomplish it, it will provide the snuggest fit for the man, leading to increased pleasure for both people. The tightness will ensure that the woman completely feels the man entering her, and the man will feel the woman's vagina hugging his penis for the entire duration of sex.

The Supine Clasping Position

The Supine Clasping Position is actually the main version of the Clasping pair and is a bit easier to engage in than The Side Clasping Position. Here, the woman will lay flat on back, with her legs straight out and pressed together. Think of yourself like a plank of wood, with your body in a perfectly straight alignment. Now, the man will lay on top of the woman, matching her position. His legs should also be straight and pressed together, resting on top of the woman's legs. His body should press down against hers, and he can place his hands on either side of her so that he can prevent her from having to bear all of his weight. The many must then enter the woman from this position, not spreading her legs at all, so that her yoni remains tightly squeezed shut.

If you are looking for depth, this position is not going to be the one for you. Because of the angle of the woman's pelvis, and the tightness of her legs, there is very little room for the man to be able to insert himself. However, if you are looking for a tight, squeezing sensation, then this position always delivers. Like with The Side Clasping Position, this is the position of Lowest Congress, so it is meant for wider women and smaller men. But, as we mentioned above, this may actually not be possible for men who are too small in length, as they will need to make up the distance that is reduced by the woman having her legs closed. Instead, this position is good for men who have more length, but possibly less width. If you fall into this category, you should find that The Supine Clasping Position is quite pleasurable for you.

The Pressing Position

The Pressing Position is less of a position, and more of a move to engage in during The Clasping Position. While the Kama Sutra does list it as its own position, it requires that you are already engaged in sex in order to complete. For this, the couple must already be engaged in either variation of The Clasping Position, although The Supine Clasping Position works best. Once you are engaged actively in sex, the woman will then use her thighs to press down tightly against the man's erection. Living up to its name, she will begin pressing tightly against it, squeezing it so as to add more pressure and tightness for him.

Pressing Position is more of a technique that a woman can utilize during sex in order to alter the sensation for both herself and her partner. It may seem unnecessary, given that The Clasping Position already offers up maximum tightness, but it is a tool at your disposal if you are looking to spice things up and play around. This move also gives the woman some control during sex, as she can effectively alter the depth and tightness to suit her desires.

Twining Position

This is another one that is listed in the Kama Sutra that is more of a technique than it is an actual position. The Twining Position can be utilized during almost all of the other sex acts, and simply consists of the woman placing her thigh over her lover's thigh. Two ways in which this can be visualized is by thinking of it in either a standing or laying down position. Beginning with laying down, if the man is on top of the woman, she can take one of her legs out from under him and bring it around the side so that her thigh is then pressed against the outside of his thigh. So long as her thigh is across his, The Twining Position is taking place. For those who enjoy sex standing up, this can easily be achieved in any standing position, regardless of whether or not you are facing each other. If you are standing face to face, the woman should lift one of her legs and place the thigh against the outside of the man's thigh. If you happen to be in a position where the woman has her back to the man, she can lift her leg and stretch it out behind her until she finds his thigh with hers.

What makes this technique so useful is that it is extremely simple and oftentimes something we already do naturally. Many positions automatically place the man and woman so that their thighs touch, so this is just being more aware of that placement. The Twining Position is perfect for enhancing the feeling of closeness, as the deliberate action of touching your bodies together connects you and you can focus on the sensation of your thighs pressed against each other.

Mare's Position

The final technique that is listed under Low Congress in the Kama Sutra is the Mare's Position. Like we saw with The Pressing Position and the Twining Position, this is in fact not a position at all and is instead a way for the woman to increase tightness during sex. What is required here is for the woman to literally trap the man's lingam inside her yoni so that he cannot remove himself. This is going to require the woman to have developed her Kegel muscles so that they are able to be engaged at her will. The Kama Sutra does make a point of saying that this technique is only learned through practice and is performed only by certain women who have been trained in this act.

Chapter 12- Advanced Tips

Sex is a composition of various movements, erogenous zones, techniques, and sensations so be assured that there are always ways to make things more amazing in the bedroom. Here are some advanced tips that can help guys and girls get the most out of each coupling.

Take Your Time

The common issue for most men with sex is that they take things too fast, failing to provide women with sufficient time to really get things in gear. Hence, she's not properly aroused and therefore unlikely to reach orgasm.

Give proper attention to the prelude or the foreplay, not just through the stimulation of the erogenous zones but also by making her comfortable and mentally ready. It is often said that the biggest and most powerful erogenous zone is the brain – which is why the Kama Sutra extensively talks about courtship and how to make the woman receptive to the advances of the male.

The Use of Sounds

Moans and other sounds coming from the female are highly arousing for many males and shows that the female is leisurely enjoying the situation. Hence, females who want to increase the satisfaction for their male partner should be vocal about the sensations they are feeling and the pleasure of the sexual act. Additional caresses, pinching, sucking, and licking aren't exclusively done by males. Women will find that performing additional tasks during sex, particularly to the erogenous zones of the male will enhance his satisfaction.

It has also been proven that men are very visual when it comes to sex. Hence, a large number of them enjoy watching the female pleasure herself during sex, either by touching her breasts or playing with the clitoris.

Alternate

The Kama Sutra talks about the need to change pace, actions, and intensity during the sexual act. The fact is that there is no specific formula for the perfect sex. Different people have different methods of enjoying the act and may require different methods for stimulation. While others are perfectly happy with the typical foreplay, others may like it better to have their lovers wearing leather or performing some service. The same is true with kissing, touching, licking, biting, and other actions. Alternating from soft to hard, fast to slow, and then vice versa can keep the passion and pleasure going, ensuring the both parties remain in the throes of sexual intensity.

You'll find that there's also no specified time length for sex. While women generally need lots of foreplay, there are situations when she is quickly and properly aroused so that there's nothing left to do but penetrate and thrust. Other times, you'd like it slow and lingering so that both parties can truly enjoy the moment. The differences and the failure to predict how the sex will occur is part of the excitement.

Talk About It

Talking about sex – whether before or after – is usually a good idea. For some couples, the conversation is done during sex. We're not talking about the 'emotional' stuff here but rather, a talk about what gets you satisfied and what doesn't. This is important because although observing the reaction of your lover is a good starting point, it doesn't always provide a clear picture of how satisfactory the sex life happens to be.

Couples are encouraged to talk about what gets them off and what sexual acts they do NOT like in the bedroom. Only through this can you perfect the sex and really get satisfaction into the bargain. Remember: every person is different so you'll have to adjust your actions depending on the person you're with.

Mirrors, Videos, and Locations

You can also further boost sexual pleasure by strategically placing mirrors in different parts of the bedroom or house so that you can watch yourself having sex. This is a big turn on for guys and actually provides a whole new dimension to the sexual union. The recording of the sex can also be terribly exciting although of course, you'll have to take careful steps to ensure that no one else views the act, especially if you have no intention of becoming a porn star.

Choosing different locations in the house to have sex in also kicks up the excitement a notch. For the most part, different locations in the house make it possible for couples to be inventive with the sexual positioning. For example, wall sex is best done in the shower while table sex can be done in the dining room. At the very least, sex in different locations of the house gives couples the chance to embed a memory into the specific location, allowing them to have something pleasant to remember each time they use the facilities.

Tips for Better Male Pleasure

The Closed Door

This position is similar to missionary in that both people are lying down face-to-face, and the man is on top. The difference, however and what makes this an advanced position is that the woman will keep her legs shut tightly the entire time. The man's penis can be inserted while her legs are open and then once it is in, she will close her legs. What this does is constrict her vagina and make the canal tighter for the man's penis. In addition to this, if she is aroused her vagina will be engorged and the canal will be tighter already. Because of this, the man's penis will be hugged closely as it slides in and out of her and this will make for extra pleasure for him.

Bend and Press

The bend and press position give the man control of the situation as the woman is lying back and receiving him. The woman will lie back on the floor or on the edge of the bed with her knees drawn up to her chest. The man then will stand close to her and slide his penis into her, leaning forward to hold her knees to her chest. This means that the woman does not have much freedom of movement, and the man is deciding the depth, the speed, and the angle at which his penis is entering her. He is likely able to achieve deep penetration in this position as her legs are lifted all the way to her chest and the man's body is holding them here, opening her body up for deeper penetration.

Legs on Shoulders

If the woman is feeling flexible and you want to try a new position that will have the man feeling great pleasure from a deeper penetration than most of the classics, try this one. The woman will lie on her back, and the man will lie on top of her, sliding his body in between her legs. Then, the woman will lift both of her legs so that each of them is on one of his shoulders. From here, he pushes his hips forward and can easily slide his penis into her vagina, which is open wide and in a perfect position for penetration. The man will do the thrusting here. This position requires flexibility from the woman but gives a deep penetration once accomplished. If she can't quite get both of her legs on his shoulders because of flexibility, she can start by lifting just one of them. She can put one leg on his shoulder and have the other one in a comfortable position beside him or around his waist. Having only one leg on his shoulder will still offer some of the benefits of a deeper penetration and you can work up to lifting both legs eventually. The man will feel great pleasure from this deep penetration as the woman's legs are open for the deepest possible penetration.

The Scissors

This position is a little difficult to get yourselves into, but once you do, it will be well worth the effort. To begin, the man will sit on the bed with his arms behind him, holding his weight up but leaning back. Then, he will bend one of his knees, so his leg is bent. The woman will lie down on the bed face-down and with her head at the opposite end of the bed as the man's. She will spread her legs and move her body toward the man's body until their bodies meet. When they meet, their bodies will look like two pairs of scissors crossed into one another. From here, the man will insert his penis into her vagina. The woman can move her body up and down on his penis and the man can thrust into her. It may take a bit of time to develop a rhythm in this position, but when you do, you will both feel intense pleasure.

Tips for better Female Pleasure

The Waterfall

The waterfall is a somewhat difficult position to get into, but once you do, it will be very pleasurable for the woman. In this position, the man has complete control, but this works in the woman's favor as he is able to focus on her entire body, leading to great amounts of pleasure for her. The man will begin by sitting in a chair with his feet on the floor. The woman will climb onto his lap, facing him and insert his penis into her. She can wrap her legs around his waist. Then, slowly she will lean all the way back until her head and arms are touching the floor. From here, the man will hold onto her hips and can move her body onto his penis at whatever speed and depth he wishes. He can also grab onto her breasts and massage her clitoris in this position, which is what makes it so pleasurable for the woman. Not only is she receiving G-Spot stimulation because of the angle at which the man's penis is entering her, she is also having her clitoris or nipples stimulated.

The Sitting Duck

The sitting duck is a position that allows the woman to have complete control. The man will lie down on the floor on his back. The woman will straddle him and slide his penis into her. Then, one by one, she will cross her legs so that she is essentially sitting on his penis cross-legged. In this position, the man has no freedom of movement, and everything is up to the woman. She can even touch her clitoris in this position if she wishes.

Chapter 13- Kama Sutra Bonus

Before diving deeply into each of the sex positions offered up the Kama Sutra, we will first begin looking at the different types of congress based on the depth of the woman's yoni (vagina) both men and women fall into three different categories based on their genital sizes, and those sizes impact what positions are ideal for each person.

For women who are deer, they have a shallower yoni, and thus they will benefit from engaging in positions that open them up to allow for better entry and depth control. Mare's fall in the middle, so the majority of positions will work fine for them. Lastly, Elephant women, who have wide yonis, benefit from engaging in positions that shrink and tighten the vagina so as to provide more stimulation and pleasure for both partners.

The Kama Sutra refers to the different positions as either High Congress or Low Congress or Equal congress. What this depends on is the pairing between the man and the woman and their personal genital sizes.

If a Deer Woman, with a shallow yoni, engages in sex with a Horse Man who is large in size, then that is High Congress. She should then ensure she is in a position that widens her so that she may accept him inside, and the ideal positions for that are the widely opened position, the yawning position, or the position of the wife of Indra.

For an Elephant Woman, with a wide yoni, who engages in sex with a Hare Man who is small in size, she is having Low Congress. This will require her to lay in a way that constricts the vagina making it tighter and shallower. Positions available for Low Congress are the clasping position, the pressing position, the twining position, and the mare's position. It is also advised that the woman uses various medicines to help her achieve orgasm, as the man's size may not be sufficient for her.

Now, Equal Congress happens when both the man's size and woman's size are equal to one another, such as an Elephant with a Horse, a Bull with a Mare, and a Hare with a Deer. In these cases, the couples may engage in sex any way they choose as all positions should lead to equal pleasure among both parties.

With regards to Mare Women, who are middle in size, the same rules apply. If a Mare engages in sex with a man who is too large, she too is engaging in High Congress and should opt for positions that open her up more widely. If she has sex with someone who is smaller in size than her, then that is Low Congress, and like with the Elephant Woman, she should attempt positions that tighten the yoni.

So, now that you have a general idea of which positions may work best for which type of person, it's time to get into the positions laid out in the Kama Sutra. We will look at what each one is, who it is best for, whether or not it is a realistic option, and many other tips and pieces of advice.

The Widely Open Position

The Widely Open Position begins with the woman laying down on her back. She should keep her head low and against the bed, while she raises up her hips so that they are higher than her head. Keeping her knees bent, her feet should not touch the ground, and instead, her knees should touch against the man's upper back. This position is designed to allow for the yoni to widen. Her partner should be kneeling between her legs, raised up so that he can meet her with his lingam. Her buttocks and lower back should rest comfortably upon his knees, while his hands grasp her sides. To bring her up higher, he may grasp on to her buttocks and raise her lower half to meet him. To increase the deepness of penetration, the woman should clasp on to the man's ankles, so that she may pull herself more tightly towards him.

This position is great for women who are with more well-endowed men, as it will open you up and allow for easier entry. But, do not think this position is only pleasurable for High Congress! Regardless of size, the Widely Open Position ensures that not much effort is exerted during sex, so that stamina for both people is increased. This is a very powerful position that can make sex last for as long as you would like it to, and neither person should find themselves getting tired quickly. It is also an intimate position, as the man gazes down upon the woman, and she gazes back up at him. Both people have their hands free if they so choose, so that they may caress each other's bodies. Men should make use of the fact that the woman's breasts are readily available to him, and he should play with them and stimulate them accordingly.

The Yawning Position

The Yawning Position has the woman begin by lying flat on her back. From here, she will need to open up her thighs as wide as possible, and then raise them in the air until her thighs are against the bed, close to the sides of the body. To assist in keeping them open, she should grasp her thighs or ankles and hold them apart. The man will then lay or kneel in between her legs and can begin penetrating her. There are a few variations that are available for this position, depending on how flexible the woman is and how the man prefers to be positioned. In the ideal situation, the woman should grasp her ankles, or her lower calves, in order to ensure her legs truly are spread wide and open. For proper Kama Sutra technique, the man will then be laying between her legs, but this can require a lot of upper body strength, as he will need to position himself on his hands or forearms to keep himself supported and this can get tiring after a while. Instead, you can alter the position by having the man kneel and lean down, which will assist with stamina.

This is another one of the positions that are listed as being ideal for High Congress, as there are few other positions that truly open up the vagina like this one. Here, the woman is as wide as she can possibly go, making deep penetration and larger penises very doable. It is an extremely intimate position, as the woman is completely exposed to her partner, and he can visually take in every part of her intimate area. For some people, this may offer too much exposure, but if you are confident enough to try it out, it can be very sensual and pleasurable. To increase the intimacy and romance, the man may lean down and kiss the woman, as the bodies are lined up perfectly for this. Both partners also face to face in this position, so you can look deeply into their eyes and connect on a more spiritual level. With that said, this position can also be extremely erotic and rough, depending on how you like to have sex. The wideness allows for fast and deep penetration, and the man can really take control here.

The Expanding Position

A slight variation from The Yawning Position also has the woman laying on her back with her legs widely spread apart. The difference that separates the two, however, is that the woman will not use her hands in order to assist her in keeping her legs apart. She may place her hands behind her head in a relaxed pose, or she may use her hands to caress the man's body. Whatever she chooses, she will need to keep her legs open naturally which can get tiring after some time. In order to offset the fatigue this position can cause, the woman can keep one leg sprawled out to the side but resting on the floor, while then raising the other leg up and away from her body. Here she will still be expanded open, but she can switch between which leg is on the ground in order to rest.

Conclusion

Thank you for making it to the end. Sexual fantasies tend to wander through our minds. The wonderful thing about sexual fantasies is that when you need to, you can call them. When you masturbate or have sex with your partner, you can conjure up sexual fantasy, that will increase your sexual excitement. But sometimes your mind gets a sexual fantasy if you expect it least. A fantasy is nothing more than an unbelievable desire, an image, or a story you carry. You can have dreams that are soothing, thrilling, or entertaining, everywhere and anywhere. There are many people who simply use their imagination to receive an intensive sexual pleasure. And more people use their imaginations and fantasies to make their sex lives exciting. It is completely normal to fantasize about anything. The choice of your fantasy is based on the use of good judgment to determine if it becomes a reality. Sexual fantasy is a good way to keep your mind (and maybe your body) motivated whether or not you have sexual fantasies for a whole day, or if you just expect the right individual in the right place and the right time to act.

The imagination or external stimuli like an attractive stranger, an erotic picture or a movie can activate fantasies. Whatever tips you give, it is good to imagine, as long as something gets you off. You can express your imagination in a sexual way through fantasies. You may think you want to do stuff, but you haven't. You can still fantasize about things you've done in the past. Or perhaps some stuff you know that never you're going to want to do, but it's still fun to think about. As often as you like you can revisit your fantasy. As if they are your own private sex retreat, you should take refuge in them. AIDS, abortion, and sexually transmitted diseases will not occur. There are other advantages of sexual imagery.

You do not need to use condoms or birth control in your imagination. In your fantasies, you can really feel liberated.

Kamasutra is yet another branch of sex which manages to fascinate most people. Once you get hooked to trying new and passionate sex positions, you might find yourself digging on Kamasutra too. A lot of Kamasutra positions might be very hard to achieve but when you have hunger and desire, nothing seems impossible.

So, re-read as many times as needed and you can always choose some of your top favorite experimental positions and please your partner in bed. Everything we have spoken assumes gargantuan importance and we hope that by reading you must have been able to bring in the much-needed change in your sex life.

Give yourself some time and keep practicing. Being a newbie at sex isn't a really bad thing. In fact, you're exploring and learning a lot of wonderful things about your partner's body as well as your own. You will one day know how to understand your partner's desires and communicate your own – even without words.

So, be willing to do your bit and bring changes for the good. When you are getting a good amount of sex and you are enjoying it, the contentment always shows on your face and this is bound to bring in a rejuvenated sense of joy in you.

CPSIA information can be obtained
at www.ICGtesting.com
Printed in the USA
BVHW040925240321
603337BV00016B/276/J

9 781914 462337